HOKUSAI

THIRTY-SIX VIEWS OF
MOUNT FUJI

HOKUSAI

THIRTY-SIX VIEWS OF
MOUNT FUJI

Amélie Balcou

PRESTEL
MUNICH · LONDON · NEW YORK

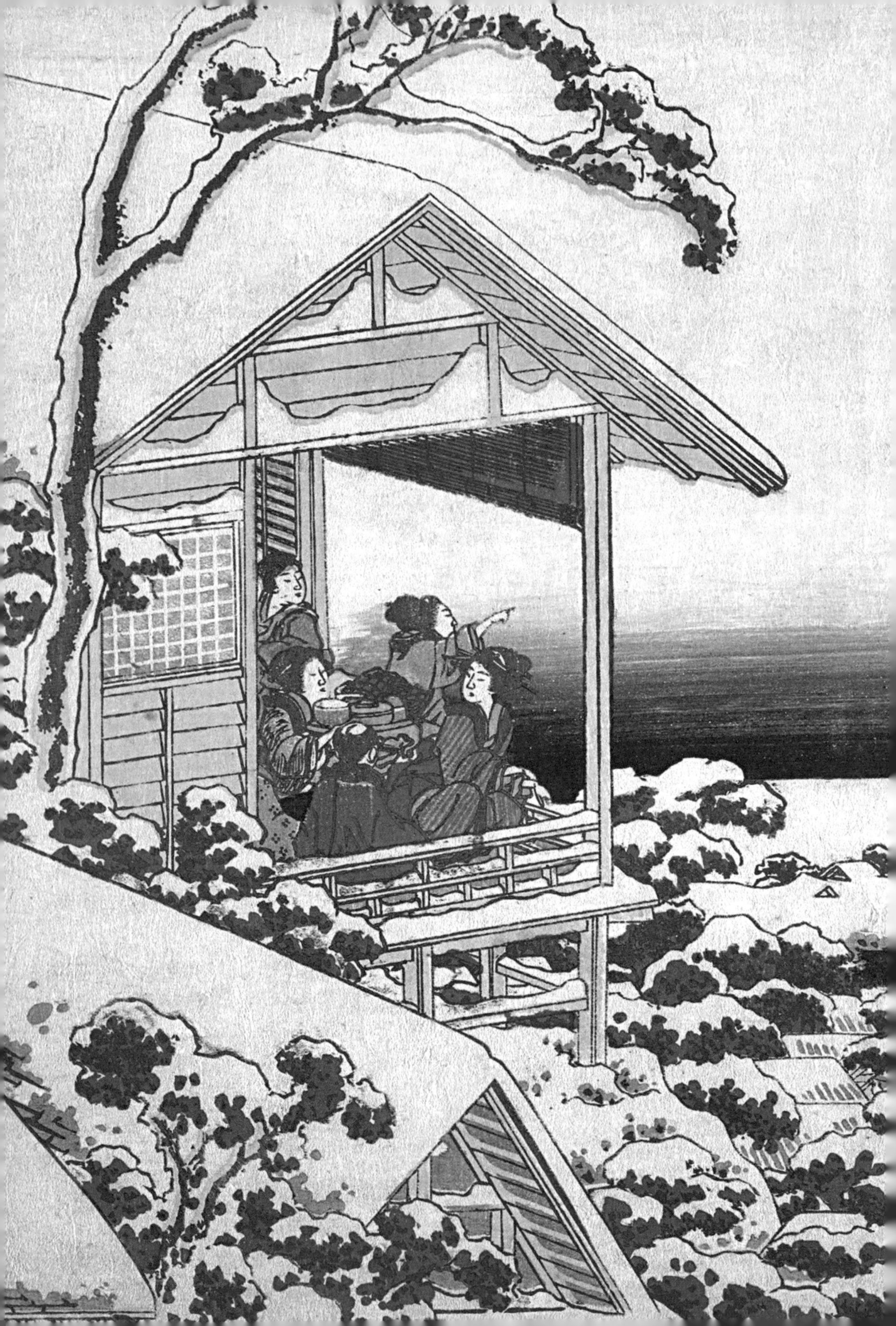

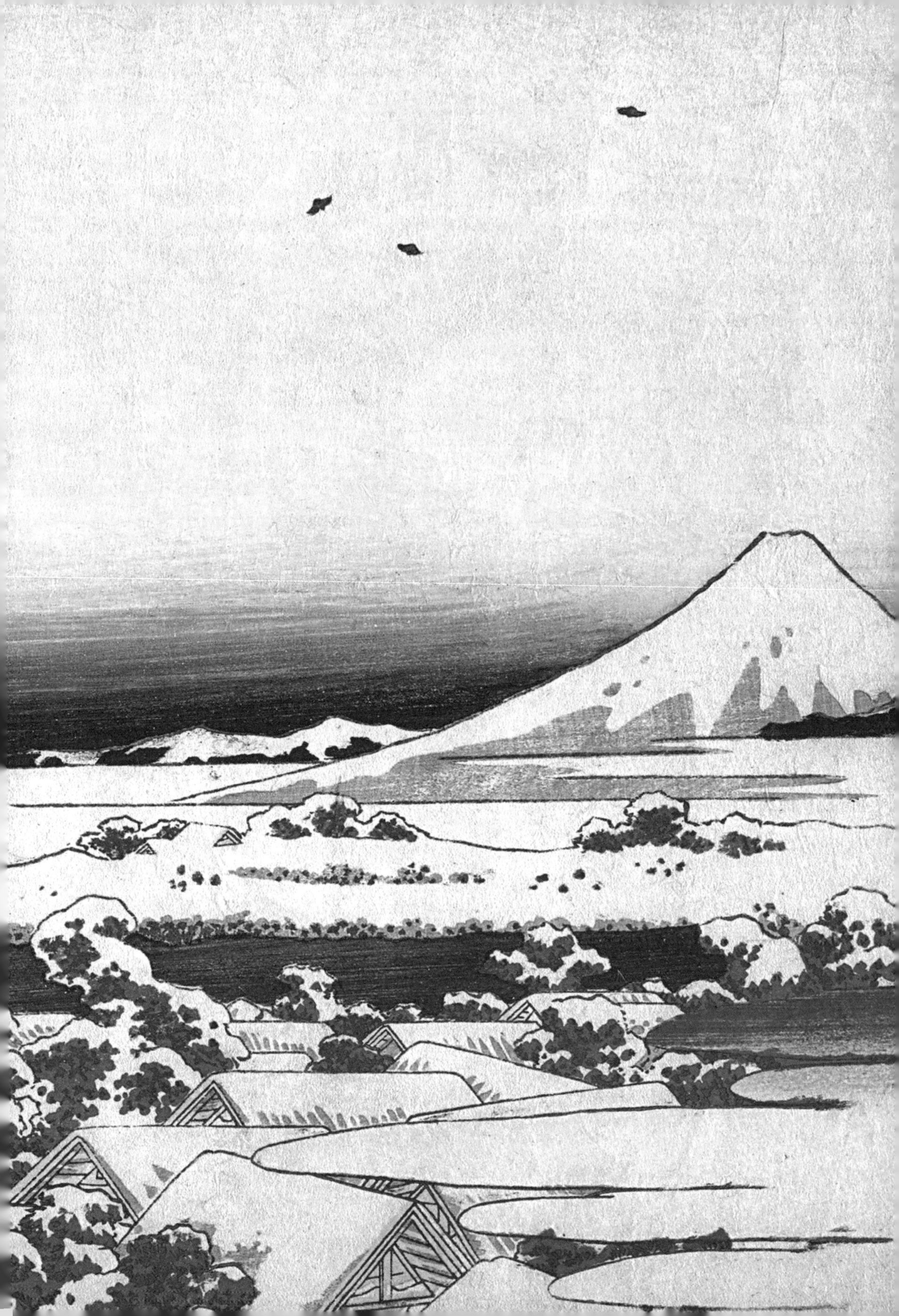

When the celebrated Japanese artist Katsushika Hokusai (1760–1849) published his famous *Thirty-Six Views of Mount Fuji* in the early 1830s, he was at the height of his career. The series took the ukiyo-e woodblock print in a radically new direction[1], focusing entirely on the landscape and presenting Mount Fuji from a variety of viewpoints and in contrasting roles – now majestic and solitary, now a mere outline on a distant horizon, now disinterestedly observing human activity. Japan's sacred volcano is seen as both impervious to the seasons – indeed, to time itself – and indifferent to the world of people, whom Hokusai playfully depicts as going about their daily lives, sometimes calmly and peacefully, in harmony with their surroundings, and sometimes at the mercy of an imposing, overpowering or even unforgiving environment.

An «old man mad about drawing», as he described himself, Hokusai delighted in contrasts. The violence of *The Great Wave off Kanagawa* is in striking opposition to the peacefulness of *Tea House at Koishikawa, the Morning after a Snowfall*, which encapsulates the fragility of life in the face of the overwhelming force of nature and the unpredictability of the elements.[2] A similar precariousness is revealed in *Kajikazawa in Kai Province*, where the fisherman perched on a rocky outcrop seems about to topple into the sea; in *The Mountains of Tōtōmi Province*, with its carpenter balancing on a wooden beam; and in *A Sketch of the Mitsui Shop in Suruga Street, Edo*, where tilers cling to a steeply sloping roof. In these prints, Hokusai captures both the eternal and the ephemeral – a fleeting moment in a human life set against the permanence of nature, forever renewed by the cycle of the seasons, and watched over by the benevolent Fuji, with its perpetually snow-capped summit. It is an opposition (or rather a juxtaposition) founded in the Buddhist principle that all worldly possessions are transitory – as represented by the storm-tossed boats in *The Great Wave off Kanagawa* – and in the Shinto belief in the omnipotence of nature.[3] And this belief certainly applies to Japan. Situated on the Ring of Fire and home to more than a hundred active volcanoes, the country is repeatedly shaken by earthquakes and eruptions.

The term ukiyo-e derives from the concept of *ukiyo*, as defined by the Japanese writer Asai Ryōi (c. 1612–1691) in his *Ukiyo Monogatari* (*Tales of the Floating World*), published in Kyoto in around 1661–1665: « Living solely in the present moment, abandoning oneself entirely to contemplation – of the moon, the snow, the cherry blossom, the maple leaves – and enjoyment, singing and drinking, simply letting oneself drift, be carried along as a calabash is carried along by a river: that is *ukiyo*, the floating world ».[4] The word conjures up a life of self-gratification, of fleeting pleasures.[5] In this sense it is close to the Roman motto *memento mori* (« Remember that you will die ») and the Homerian *carpe diem* (« Seize the day »).

Our life in this world –
to what shall I compare it?
It is like a boat
rowing out at break of day,
leaving not a trace behind.

Sami Mansei *(Man'yōshū)*

In *Thirty-Six Views of Mount Fuji*, Hokusai's vision – and that of his publisher Nishimura Yohachi – was on a grand scale. It was one of the first great series of large, landscape-format prints[6] dedicated entirely to scenic views. Admittedly, mountains – and particularly Mount Fuji – had featured in ukiyo-e since ancient times; the great volcano, whose ominous presence was both venerated and feared, had been widely celebrated in literature and painting since the 8th century, a period in which it was especially active. Hokusai himself was a master of dramatic and exotic landscapes and, like many earlier artists, had painted natural scenes throughout his long and prolific career, including several in the Chinese *sansui-ga* («images of mountains and water») style, which had developed 70 years before the appearance of *Thirty-Six Views*. In the early 1800s he had also attempted a series of landscape paintings using Western principles of perspective, *Eight Views of Edo in the Dutch Style*. Until then, however, the landscape had been of only secondary importance in ukiyo-e, and its promotion to principal subject, as well as Hokusai's stylised treatment of it, made his new series profoundly innovative.

In *Thirty-Six Views of Mount Fuji*, Hokusai skilfully manipulates geometric shapes and cleverly combines Western perspective with traditional Japanese pictorialism. In *Fine Wind, Clear Morning* (also known as *South Wind, Clear Sky* and *Red Fuji*), the mountain dominates the composition, which is typical of the traditional ukiyo-e style – and of the Chinese art that strongly influenced it – in lacking both a horizon and a vanishing point.[7] In contrast, *Nihonbashi Bridge in Edo* is composed in accordance with the principles of Western perspective, while in *A Sketch of the Mitsui Shop in Suruga Street, Edo*, in *Sazai Hall – Temple of Five Hundred Rakan* and in *Yoshida on the Tōkaidō*, Mount Fuji becomes the focal point of the composition. In his attempt to create images that were both harmonious and realistic, Hokusai uses symmetry and asymmetry, straight and diagonal lines, stasis and movement, light and shade, incorporating them into fluid shapes and colours whose freshness is heightened by the artist's frequent and extensive use of Prussian blue. First imported into

Japan in 1829, this artificial pigment, manufactured in the Netherlands, was far richer and more intense than the natural dyes used until then – so much so that Nishimura Yohachi was immediately prompted to publish a supplementary edition of *Thirty-Six Views*, alongside the standard colour prints, in *aizuri-e*, i.e. predominantly in Prussian blue.[8] Although Hokusai's aim was to create subtle and atmospheric scenes, the new pigment allowed him to provide extra luminosity to the sky and the sea.

Thirty-Six Views was an instant success, and Yohachi asked for 10 more prints of Fuji seen from the other side (although Hokusai did not restrict himself to views of the north face of the mountain), which were added after the first printing. Landscapes of this kind appealed particularly to the *chōnin*, the urban middle-class, who were the principal buyers of prints at the time. By the mid-19th century, *the Tokugawa Shogunate (1603–1867[9])*, which in 1641 had instituted the policy of *Sakoku* (« closed country ») and subsequently restricted movement even within Japan, was in decline. The flow of edicts and regulations that had so needlessly stifled the country for almost two centuries lessened, and people were at last permitted to circulate freely.[10] Moreover, the development throughout the Tokugawa period of the country's major roads, linking the cities of Tokyo (then Edo), Kyoto and Osaka, made travelling – whether for pleasure or for pilgrimages to the various monasteries and sanctuaries in the surrounding countryside – both simpler and safer.[11] As a result, the Japanese began to explore the country, reconnecting with the natural world, seeking out spectacular scenery, waterfalls and lakes, and rediscovering ancient traditions, in accordance the precepts of Buddhism and Shintoism.

The publication of *Thirty-Six Views* not only turned landscape into a major theme of ukiyo-e, but also revitalised the art of woodblock printing at a time of official censorship[12], when a number of those who spoke out against it were arrested and imprisoned (the kabuki actor *Ichikawa Danjūrō VII* was expelled from Edo, and the writers *Ryūtei Tanehiko a*nd Tamenaga Shunsui were driven to suicide). A series of edicts revised the rules relating to such prints, banning the publication of erotic *shunga* (literally « spring pictures ») and images of actors and courtesans, and even limiting the number of colours that could be used. Although many artists found ways around these restrictions – for example by depicting actors « anonymously » (Utamaro concealed the identity of his models by the use of puzzles)[13] or by passing theatrical tableaux off as scenes from fiction or legend – the Japanese print gradually lost its vitality in the face of the numbing conservatism of the Tokugawa shoguns, who throughout the Edo period subjected the people to a puritanical regime based on Confucianism.[14]

Thus, under Hokusai's influence, ukiyo-e, or the art of Japanese woodblock printing, began to focus on landscape and the depiction of daily life. Hiroshige soon also found success in this genre with his *Fifty-Three Stations of the Tōkaidō*, published in 1833/1834, and in the latter year Hokusai began his *One Hundred Views of Mount Fuji*, as well as several other landscape series, such as *Wondrous Views of Famous Bridges in All the Provinces* and *A Tour of the Waterfalls of the Provinces*, in which he adopted the theme of *setsu gekka* (« snow, moon and flowers ») from Chinese art in representations of spring (flowers), autumn (moon) and winter (snow).[15] His last great series, *True Mirror of Chinese and Japanese Poems* and *The Hundred Poems Told by the Nurse*, whose titles are but pretexts for further exploration of the landscape in both its picturesque and its spiritual aspects, also reveal the extent of Hokusai's identification with nature – as exemplified by the short poem he wrote in the year he died:[16]

Now as a spirit
I shall roam
The summer fields

[1] Jocelyn BOUQUILLARD, *Hokusai: Les Trente-Six Vues du Mont Fuji*, Paris, Seuil, 2010, pp. 7–13; Laure DALON, *Hokusai*, exhibition catalogue (Grand Palais, Paris, 1st October 2014–18th January 2015), Paris, Réunion des musées nationaux, 2014, p. 282.

[2] Jocelyn BOUQUILLARD, *op. cit.*

[3] *Ibid.*

[4] Hélène BAYOU, *Images du Monde flottant. Peintures et estampes japonaises xviie-xviiie siècles*, Paris, Réunion des musées nationaux, 2004, p. 20; Donald Jenkins, « The Roots of Ukiyo-e: Its Beginnings to the Mid-Eighteenth Century », in *The Hotei Encyclopedia of Japanese Woodblock Prints*, Amsterdam, Hotei Publishing, 2005, pp. 47–74.

[5] *Ibid.*

[6] The paper size is known as *ôban*, measuring roughly 26 × 38 cm.

[7] Nelly DELAY, *L'Estampe japonaise*, Paris, Hazan, 2004, pp. 201–257.

[8] *Ibid.*

[9] Also known as the Edo period.

[10] *Ibid.*

[11] Jocelyn BOUQUILLARD, *op. cit.*

[12] During the Tenpō Era (1830–1845), culminating in the Tenpō Reforms, instituted by a Chief Councillor of the Tokugawa Shogunate, Mizuno Tadakuni, in 1842; see Jocelyn Bouquillard, op. cit.

[13] Sarah E. THOMPSON, « Censorship and Ukiyo-e prints. Japanese Woodblock Prints », in *The Hotei Encyclopedia of Japanese Woodblock Prints*, Amsterdam, Hotei Publishing, 2005, pp. 318–322; Nelly Delay, *op. cit.*, pp. 57–59.

[14] There had been two other major clampdowns earlier in the Edo period: the Kyōhō Reforms of 1716–1736 and the Kansei Reforms of the 1790s; see Sarah E. Thompson, *op. cit.*

[15] Christine SHIMIZU, « Seasons and Places in Yamato Landscape and Painting », *Ars Orientalis*, vol. 12, 1981, pp. 1–18; C. Shimizu, « La nature et les saisons dans la peinture japonaise », in C. Shimizu (ed.), *Le Japon au fil des saisons : collection Robert et Betsy Feinberg*, exhibition catalogue (Musée Cernuschi, Paris, 19th September 2014–11th January 2015), Paris, Paris Musées, 2014, pp. 31–37.

[16] Nelly DELAY, *op. cit.*, pp. 201–257.

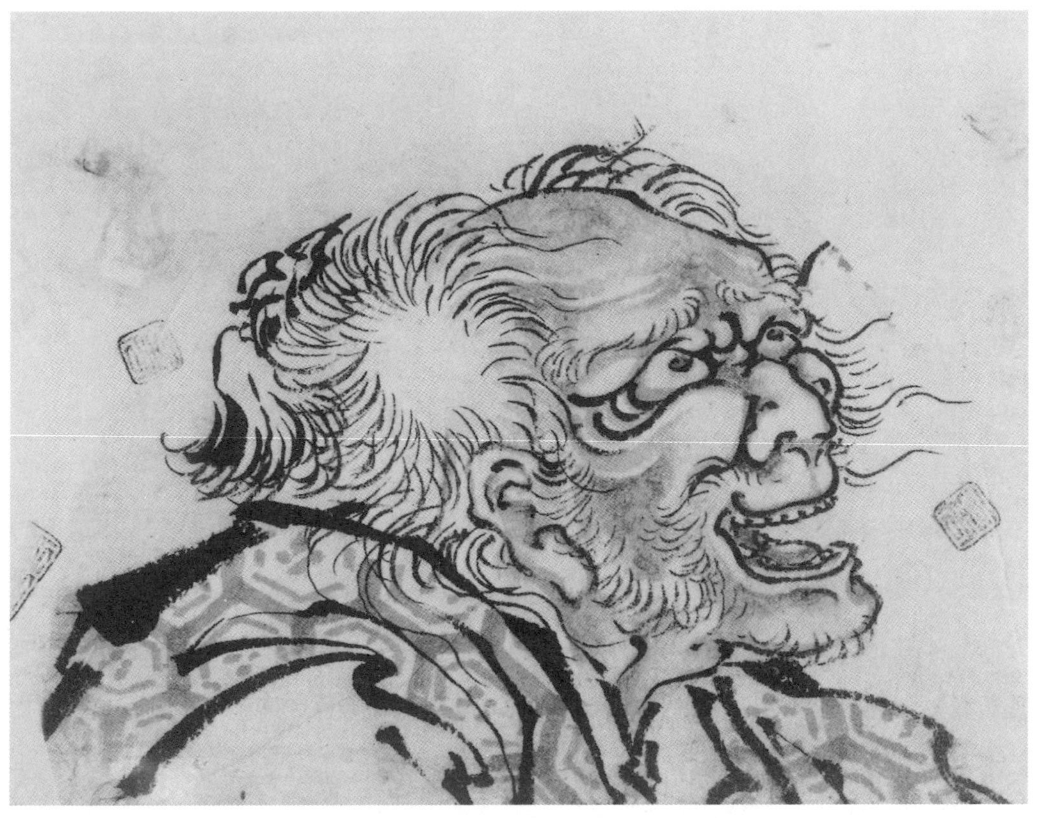

Self-portrait (c. 1840)
Woodcut printed in ink on paper

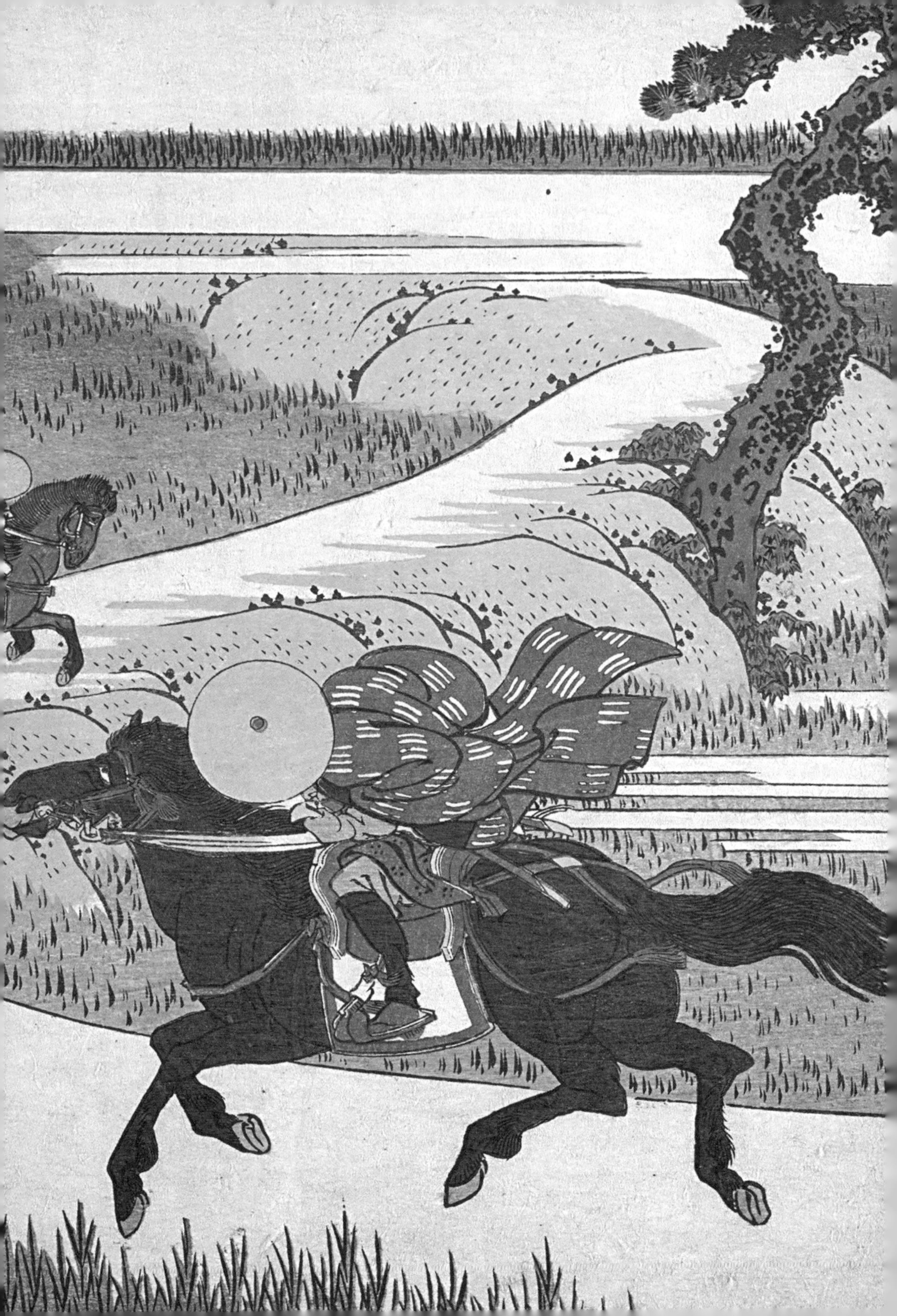

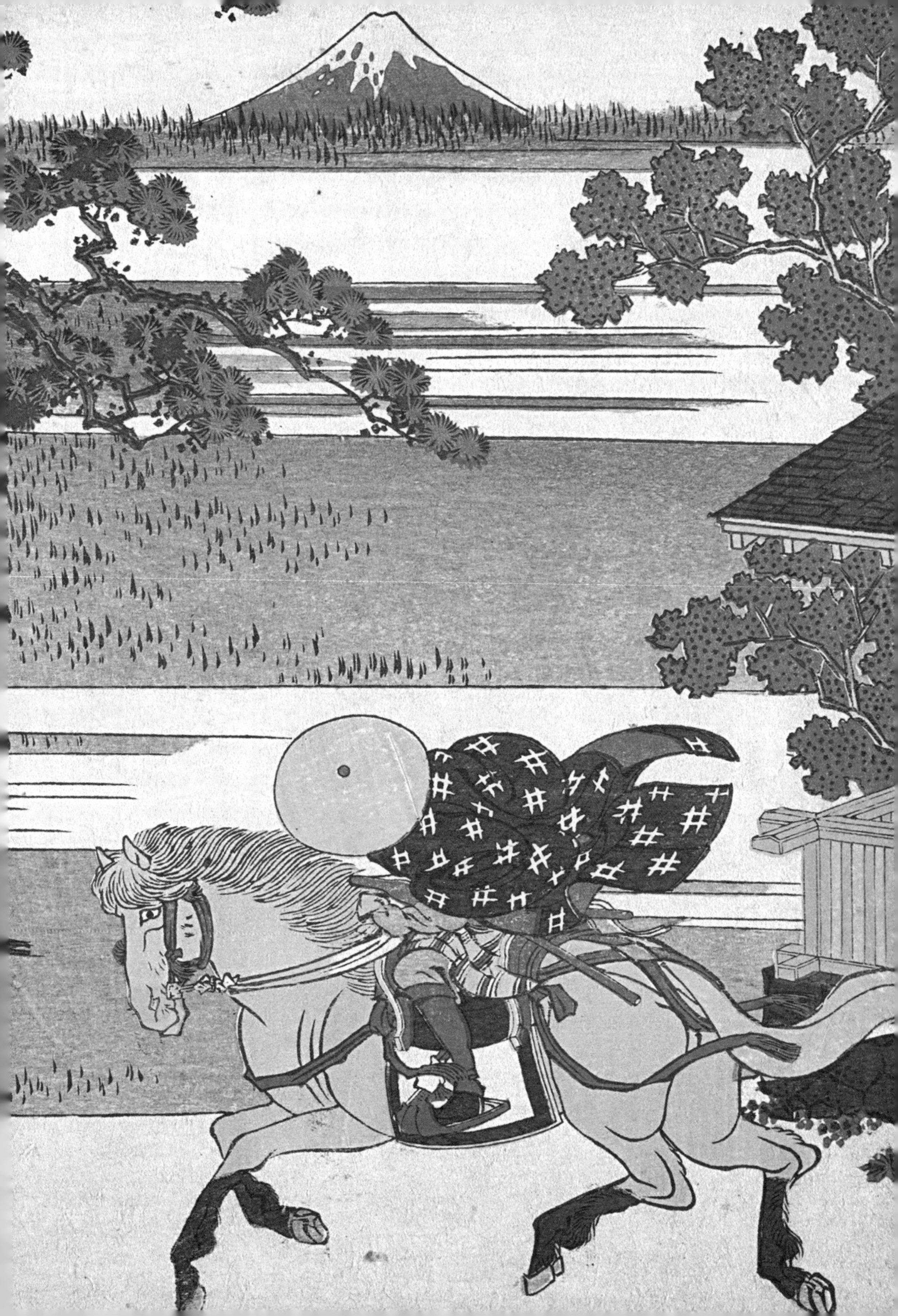

View 1
The Great Wave off Kanagawa

The quintessential Hokusai print, *The Great Wave off Kanagawa* is powerful curtain-raiser to the series. Awesome and majestic, yet also cruel and
pitiless, the breaking wave crashes violently onto three fishing boats. The
fragility of human life is contrasted with the supreme force of nature –
both eternal and unpredictable – as Mount Fuji looks on imperturbably.

View 2
Fine Wind, Clear Morning (also known as *South Wind, Clear Sky* and *Red Fuji*)

The mythical mountain stands before us like a great ruler – noble and
powerful – in a typically minimalist Japanese composition, without perspective. Uncharacteristically, Hokusai excludes the human element,
concentrating instead on the presence of the sacred mountain itself.
Crimson in the morning sunlight, the imposing volcano is set off against
a deep blue sky, dotted with stylised white clouds.

View 3
Rainstorm Beneath the Summit

This two-dimensional composition is similar to the previous view, but
here Hokusai depicts Mount Fuji in stormy weather. Its summit, dark-
ened by the storm, emerges impassively from a misty gloom torn apart
by bright red flashes of lightning. Widely associated with the element
of fire, the sacred mountain is shown here as master of nature's destruc-
tive force.

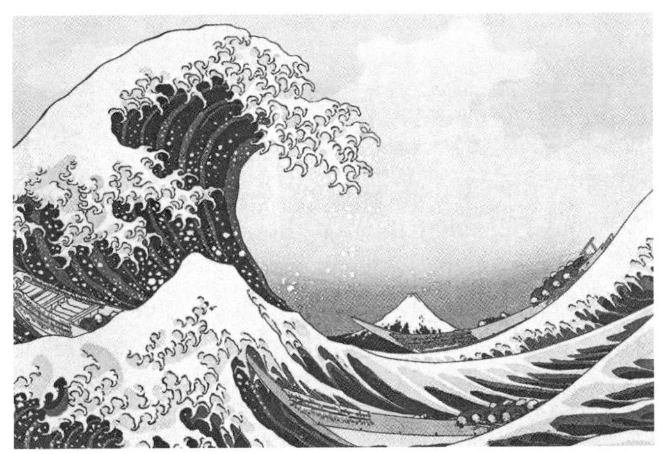

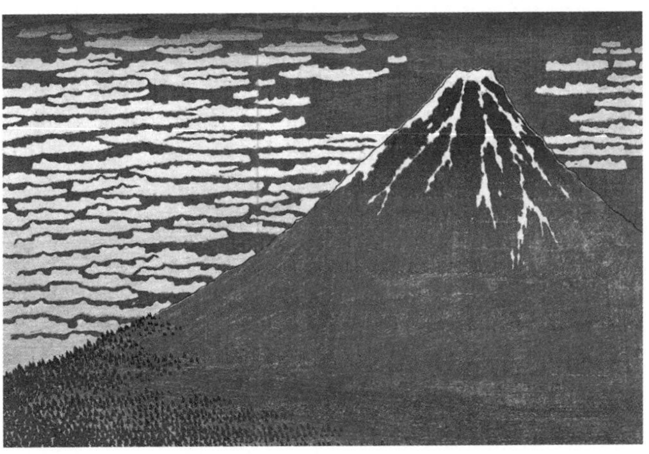

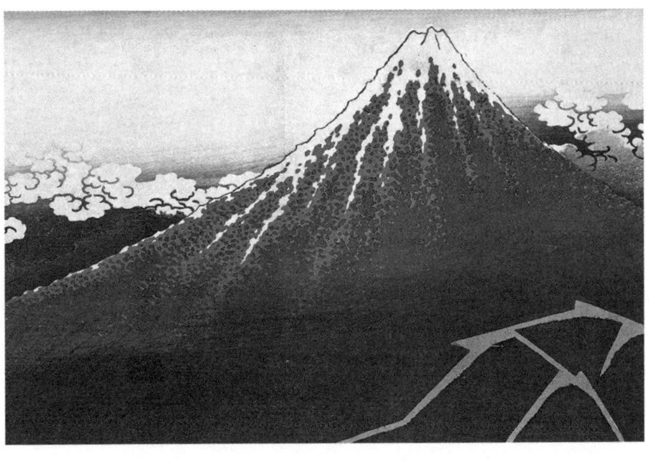

View 4
Under Mannen Bridge at Fukagawa

A boat laden with produce is steered between the piers of the Mannen-bashi (« the ten-thousand-year-old bridge ») straddling the Fuka river, on its way out into the Sumida. Hokusai exaggerates the curve of the bridge, bustling with people, and depicts the buildings beyond in playful perspective. In the distance, to the left of the tower of a fire station, stands Mount Fuji, dominating the banks of the great river.

View 5
Sundai, Edo

Workers and travellers make their way through the district of Sundai in Edo (today officially Kanda-Surugadai, in Tokyo). On the paved path leading down to the Sumida river, a samurai and his three servants pass workmen, pilgrims and travelling salesmen laden with bags and boxes.

View 6
Cushion Pines at Aoyama

Near a forest of verdant pines, a group of pilgrims stop to picnic on a rocky promontory in the zen gardens of Kyoto's Ryōan-ji Temple and to enjoy the fine weather. Walking along the steep, winding path leading to the Buddhist temple, a man draws his son's attention to Mount Fuji, half hidden by a layer of mist.

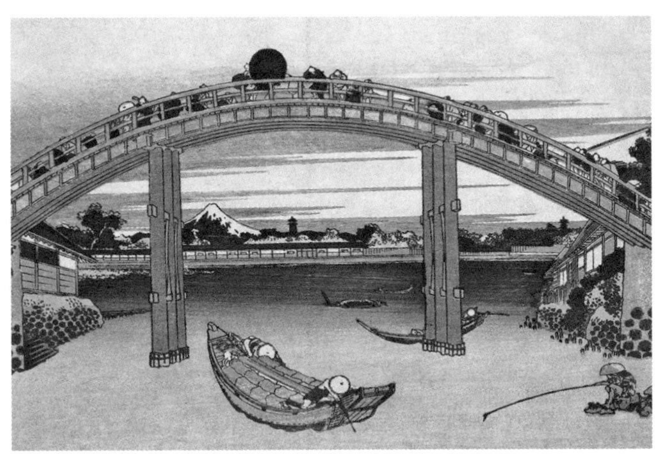

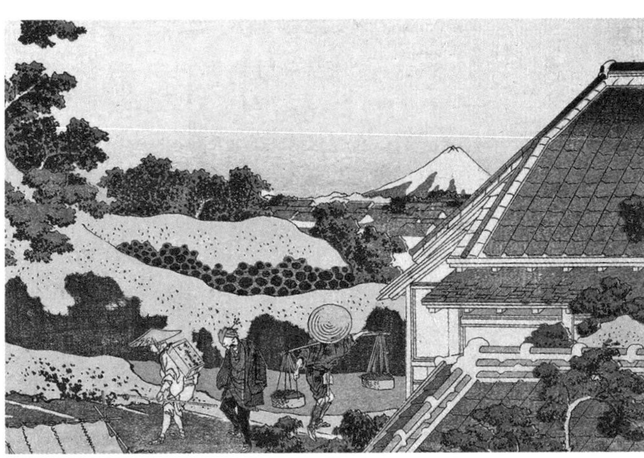

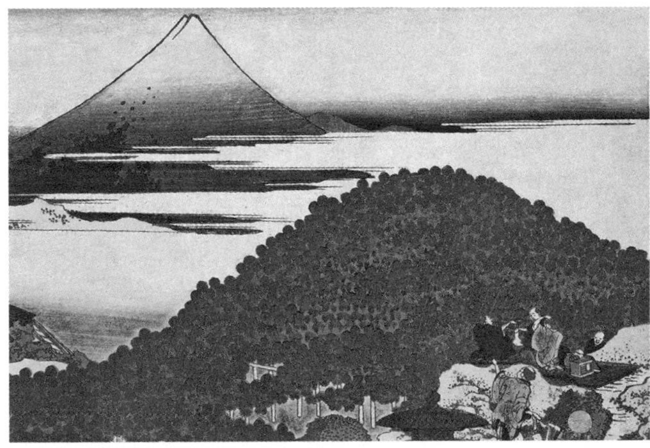

View 7
Senju in Musashi Province

As he passes two fishermen in Senju, a northern suburb of Edo, a peasant lifts his *kasa* to admire Mount Fuji, rising from the skyline behind the tall frame of a house under construction. The man is leading a horse whose saddlebags are full of grass, and attached to its lead rope is a small tortoise, which the peasant has probably picked up along the way.

View 8
Tama River in Musashi Province

Against a simple backdrop of Mount Fuji emerging from the mist, fishermen drift on the Tama river, while in the foreground a peasant leads his packhorse, as in the previous view. Hokusai restricts his palette here, concentrating on the use of Prussian blue to lend the scene a peaceful, almost serene atmosphere.

View 9
Inume Pass in Kai Province

As the setting sun turns the sky to shades of ochre, two travellers make their way past Mount Fuji along the lush green Inume Pass. Below them, two traders, with their heavily laden horses, look as though they will have difficulty climbing the steep hill ahead.

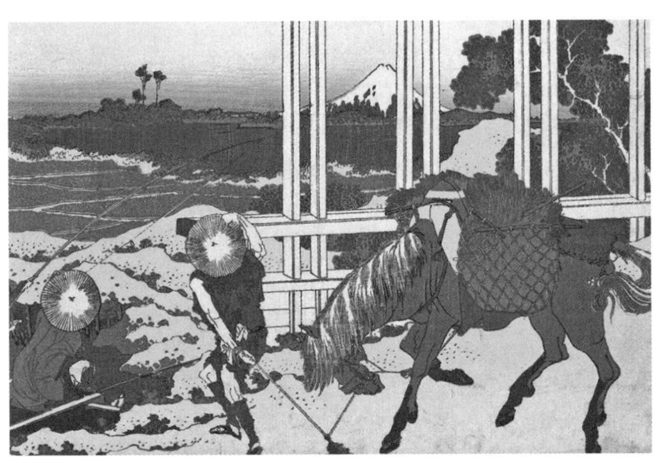

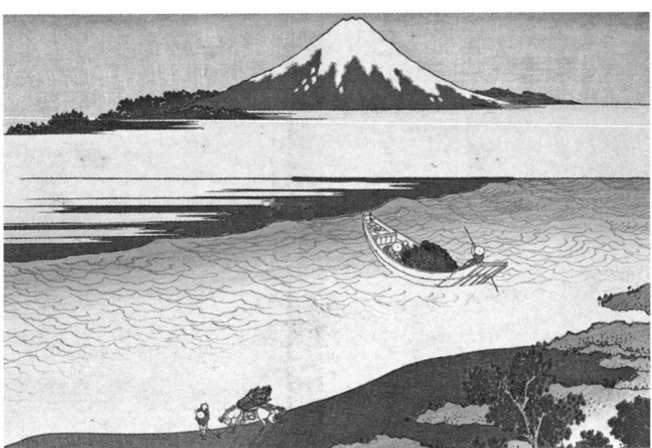

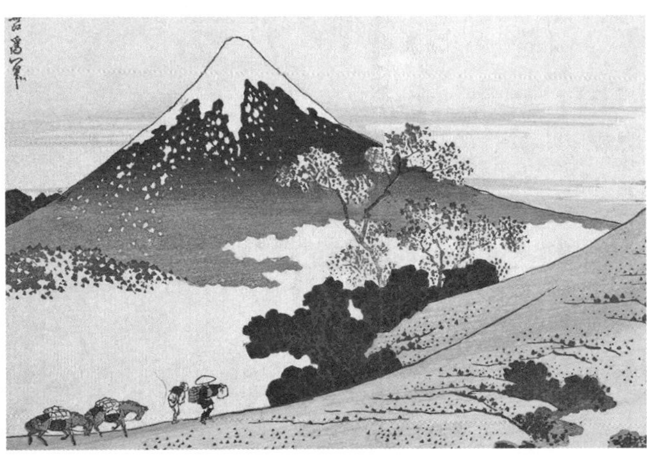

View 10
The « Fuji-View Fields » in Owari Province

The distant blue-and-white outline of Mount Fuji's summit peeks out
from behind a lush forest, as a craftsman makes a huge barrel out of
wooden planks. Half-naked, he hunches over his task, an assortment of
tools scattered about him on the bright green grass.

View 11
Asakusa Hongan-ji Temple in Edo

Mount Fuji is again shrouded in mist as workmen repair the elaborate
roof of the 17th-century Hongran-ji Temple in Edo (Tokyo). On the
left, a wooden scaffolding that serves as a fire look-out tower rises from
a cluster of houses, above which a kite, symbolising the new year, floats
in the breeze.

View 12
Tsukuda Island in Musashi Province

In summer, the fishing village on the tiny island of Tsukuda, near
the capital, is a hive of activity. A large wasen loaded with produce,
surrounded by fishing boats crowding the Sumida estuary, draws us into
the composition, the masts of sailing boats leading the viewer's eye up
into the sky.

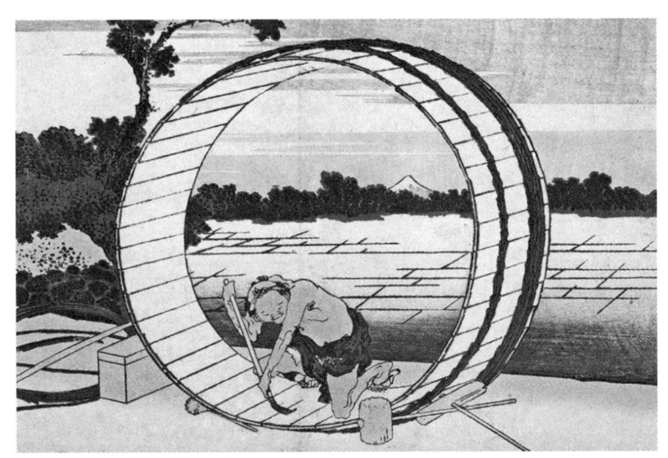

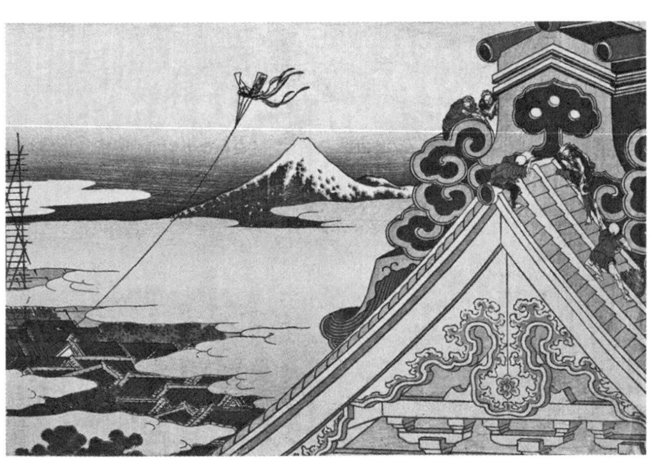

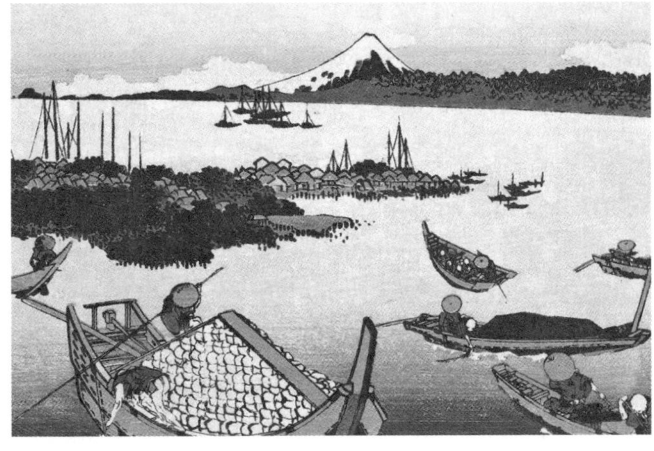

View 13
Shichiri Beach in Sagami Province

Here Mount Fuji is seen from the coastal region of Shichiri. The sacred
mountain blends into a rocky, wintry landscape depicted in blue, green
and white. Down in the fog-carpeted valley, a few dilapidated houses,
their thatched roofs covered in snow, betray the presence of a tiny fishing village.

View 14
The Marshes of Umezawa in Sagami Province

In this view, Hokusai associates Mount Fuji with a sacred bird of Japan
and symbol of longevity, the crane. In the foreground, and appearing
completely out of scale, five cranes wade in a pond, under the watchful
eye of the volcano, which looks down from among the clouds like the
king of the gods, its slopes delineated in shades of Prussian blue.

View 15
Kajikazawa in Kai Province

Perched on a rocky outcrop, as if about to plunge into the void, a fisherman clings to his lines, which the stormy sea seems to be dragging away
from him. Behind him, a small boy sits cross-legged by a wicker basket, waiting to receive the catch. Inspired by the great Chinese artists,
Hokusai contrasts the detailed drawing of the foreground with the bare
outline of Mount Fuji in the background.

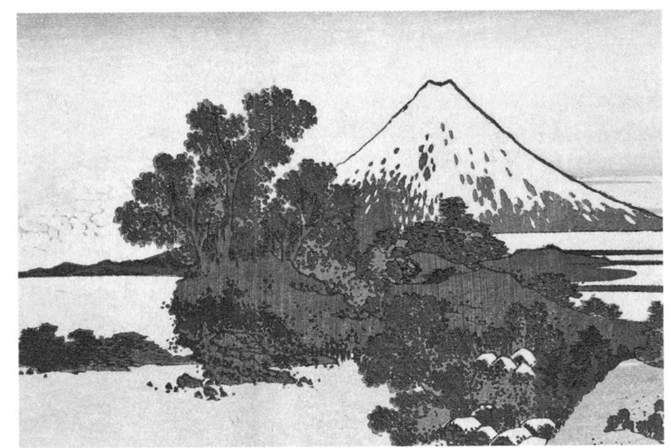

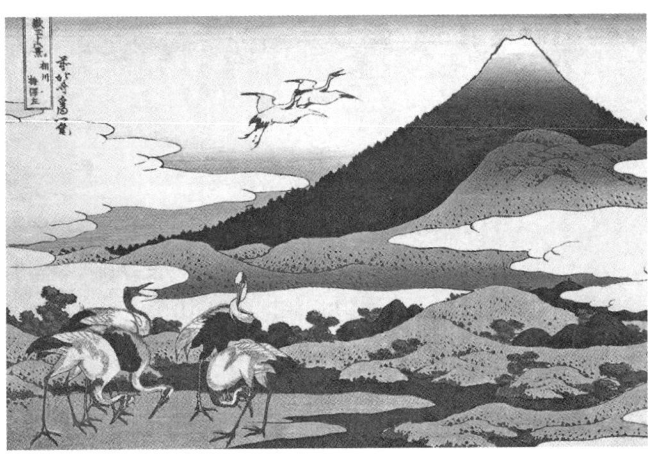

冨嶽三十六景　相州梅澤左
前北斎為一筆

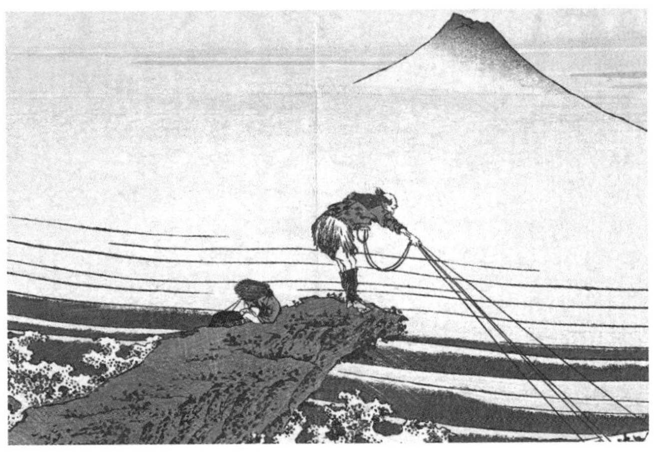

View 16
Mishima Pass in Kai Province

At the foot of Mount Fuji, its summit topped with smoke, a group of travellers rest by a massive cedar. While one of them sits smoking his pipe, three others extend their arms around the tree's trunk, as if to measure its circumference (or perhaps in worship). Below, other travellers continue down the steep path.

View 17
Lake Suwa in Shinano Province

Here Hokusai offers a distant view of Mount Fuji from behind a tiny hut, perched on a rocky outcrop above Lake Suwa. Just below the mountain is Takashima Castle, jutting out over the water from the town of Shimosuwa. In this *aizuri-e* print, the scene is like a study in Prussian blue.

View 18
Ejiri in Suruga Province

Travellers on the Tōkaidō (« Eastern Sea Route ») – here a winding path between the rice fields of Ejiri, in Suruga Province – are caught by a violent gust of wind. Unmoved by the scene, Mount Fuji in the background is barely outlined against a pink autumnal sky.

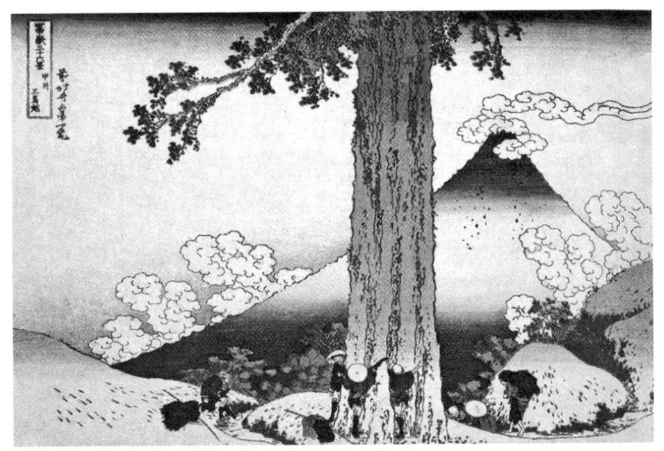

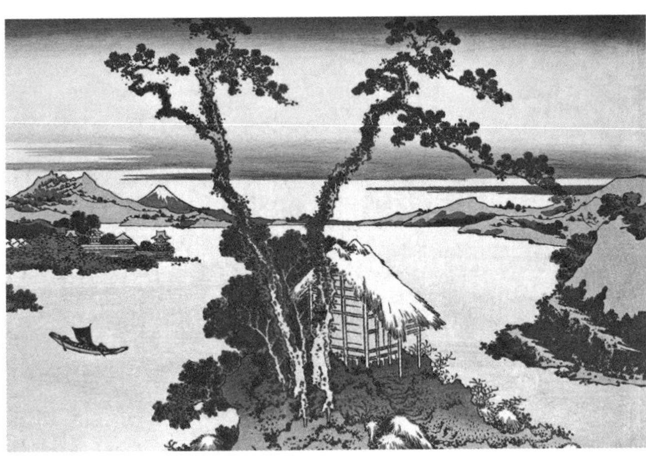

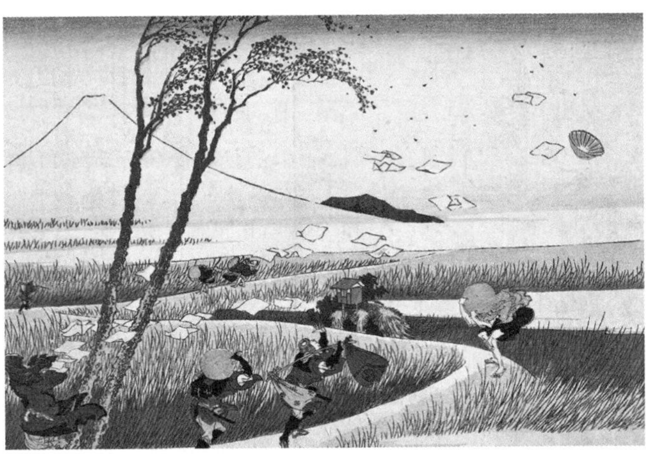

View 19
The Mountains of Tōtōmi Province

Carpenters are at work in a lumber yard in the Tōtōmi Mountains.
While two of them slice up a massive beam, another, watched by a
woman with a baby on her back, sits on a bamboo mat, sharpening his
saw, and a fourth, in the centre of the picture, takes time out to observe
the wisps of smoke billowing around Mount Fuji.

View 20
Ushibori in Hitachi Province

Hokusai presents a finely detailed picture of a junk that has been con-
verted into a home and moored among the reeds near the port of Ushibori on Lake Kasumigaura. On the left of this winter scene, printed
in cool colours, two herons fly off, as one of the occupants of the junk
empties a container in which he has probably just cooked some rice.

View 21
A Sketch of the Mitsui Shop in Suruga Street, Edo

Balancing precariously on the sloping roof, workers repair the tiles of
the Mitsui textile emporium on this shopping street in Edo. Signs on
other shops advertise the goods on offer, the prices and the payment
terms – cash only!

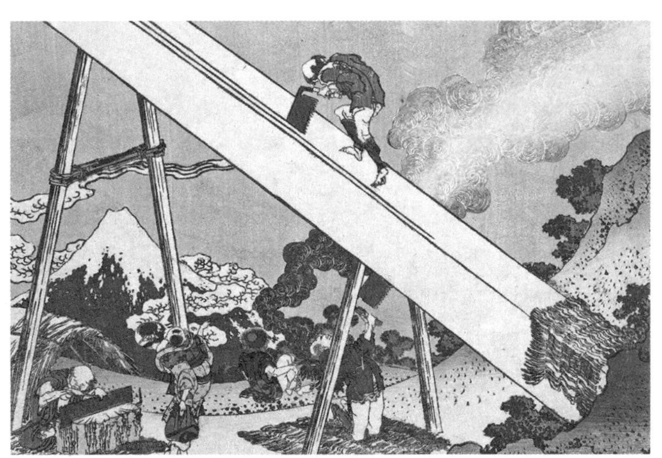

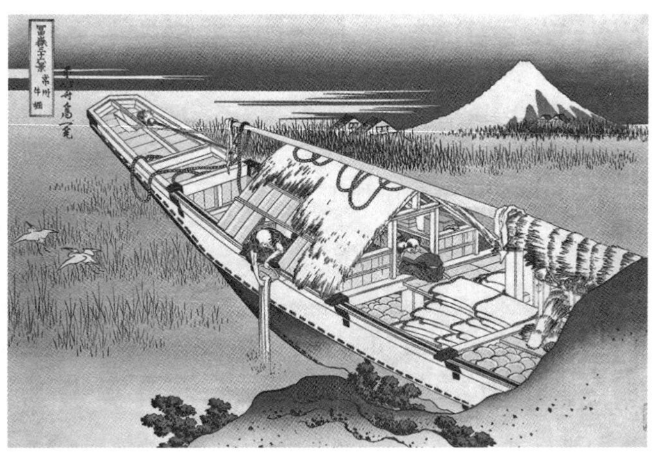

冨嶽三十六景
常州牛堀
前北斎為一筆

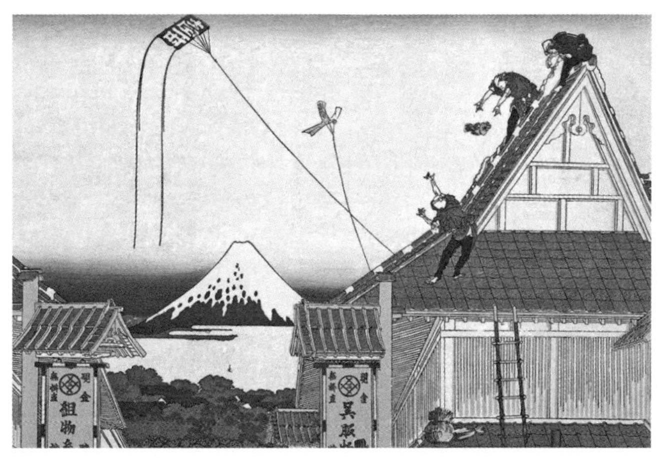

粗物立
其服山

View 22

Sunset across the Ryōgoku Bridge from the Bank of the Sumida River at Onmayagashi

A ferry heading out towards the Ryōgoku bridge and Mount Fuji carries passengers from all walks of life: samurai and salesmen, tourists and travellers, women and monks. Some, including the pilot, look at the sacred mountain, while one man slumps in the bow and another lets a piece of cloth trail in the water – a gesture echoing that of the woman doing her washing on the left in the picture.

View 23

Sazai Hall – Temple of the Five Hundred Rakan

Pilgrims at the Temple of the Five Hundred Rakan (guardians of Buddhist law) enjoy a sunny view of Mount Fuji from the terrace of Sazai Hall. While two exhausted porters set down their heavy loads, a young man points enthusiastically at the volcano, to the right of which the wooden piles of a construction site tower over the countryside, where one or two houses nestle among the trees.

View 24

Tea House at Koishikawa the Morning after a Snowfall

A group of travellers on the terrace of a tea house in the village of Koishikawa, seen almost from behind, admire Mount Fuji, now covered in snow. As a waitress appears with a tray full of food, a young woman points eagerly at a flock of birds.

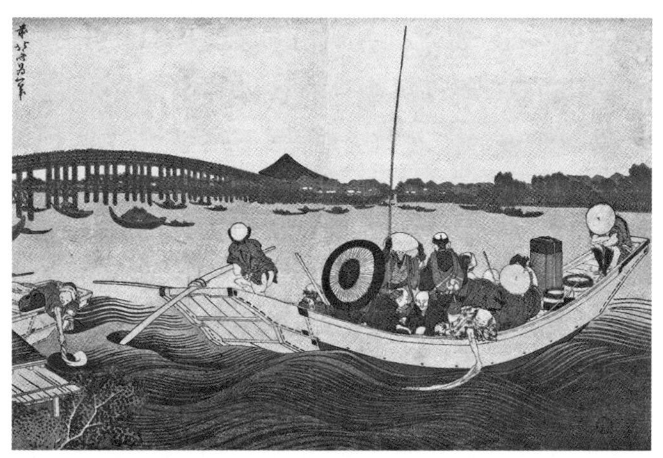

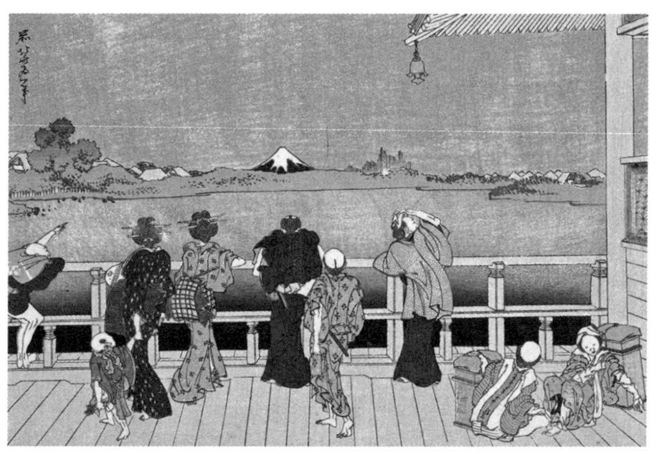

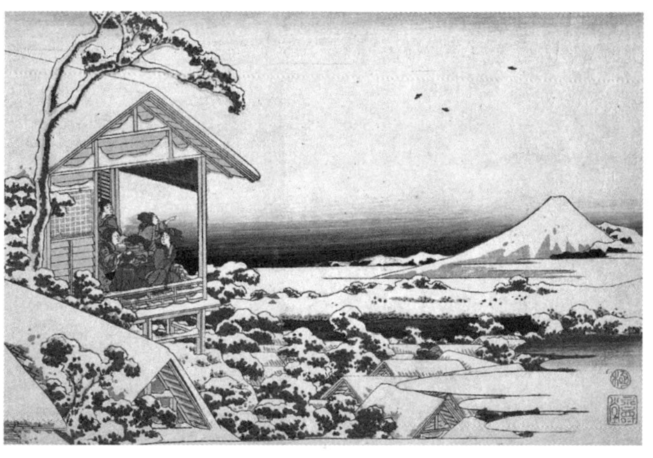

View 25
Lower Meguro

The village of Meguro in the suburbs of Edo, a favourite spot for fal-
conry, is the setting Hokusai chooses for this rural scene. Amid the ter-
raced paddy fields, thatched roofs and haystacks, hunters and country
folk go about their business without paying any attention to the distant
volcano, which Hokusai merely sketches in behind the steep hills.

View 26
The Watermill at Onden

Country people bring their rice to the watermill on the Shibuya river
in the village of Onden for hulling and washing. The men carry the
heavy sacks of freshly harvested rice up the hill, while the women wash
the hulled rice using a bucket and a basket. Beside them is a child with
a pet tortoise.

View 27
Enoshima in Sagami Province

Pilgrims file over the sandy causeway across Sagami Bay to reach the
island of Enoshima and worship at the famous Shrine of Benzaiten,
goddess of music and the arts, and of luck and love. On the right,
Mount Fuji is silhouetted against a misty orange sky.

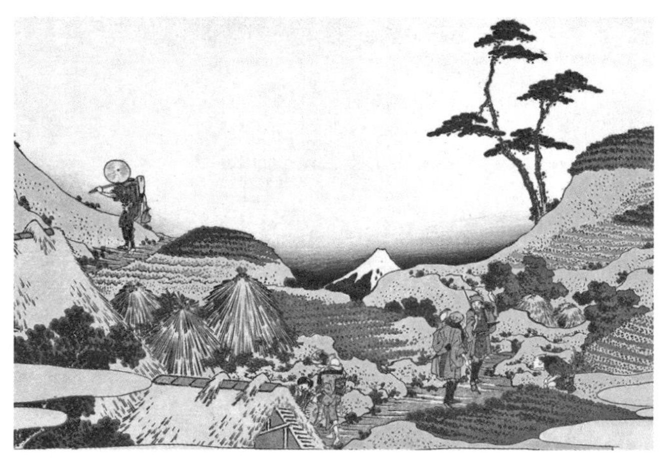

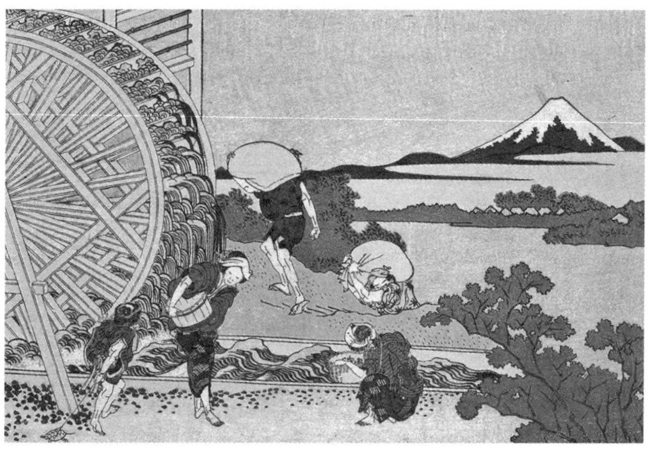

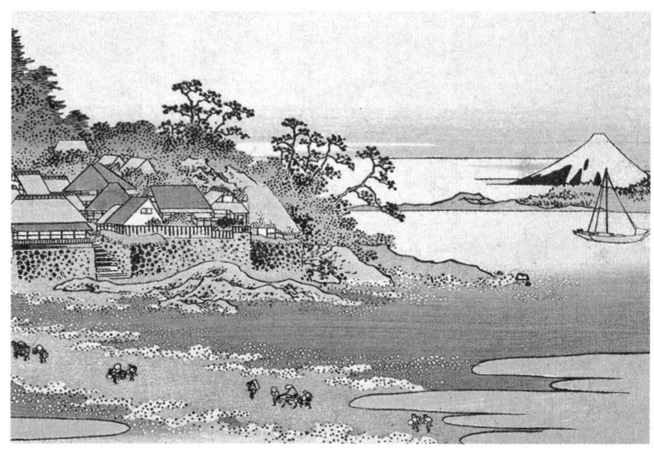

View 28
Tago Bay near Ejiri on the Tōkaidō

Partly obscured by stylised layers of mist, Mount Fuji towers over a
group of fishing boats. Rowers struggle to keep them steady while men
perched on the bows haul in the nets. On the beach, people from the
village of Ejiri (the 18th Station of the Tōkaidō) gather salt.

View 29
Yoshida on the Tōkaidō

Travellers enjoy the view of Mount Fuji from the bay window of a tea
house at Yoshida (the 34th Station of the Tōkaidō), over which hangs
a sign reading *«Fujimi chaya»* («tea house with a view of Fuji»). While
a waitress points out the volcano to two lady customers, their porters,
relieved of their burdens, take a well-earned rest. In the foreground, an
old man crouches beside a palanquin, beating a shoe with a mallet to
soften the leather.

View 30
Off the Coast of Kazusa Province

Two impressive cargo boats, their sails billowing in the wind and passengers safely below decks, cross the sea off Kazusa Province. In the distance, Mount Fuji can be seen just over the curved horizon. (The idea
that the earth was round was already widely known in Japan, thanks to
its trading with the Dutch.)

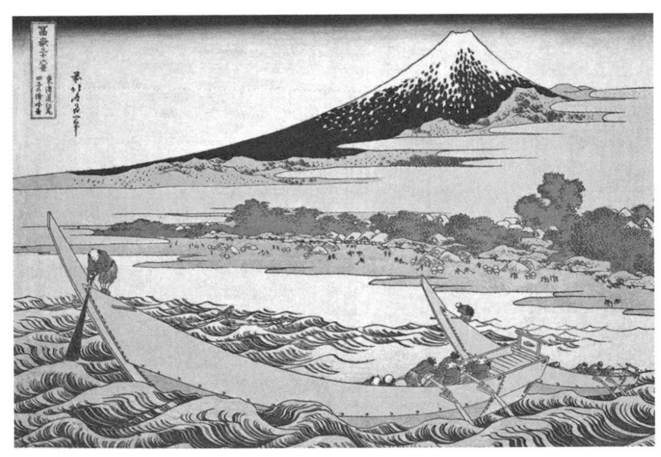

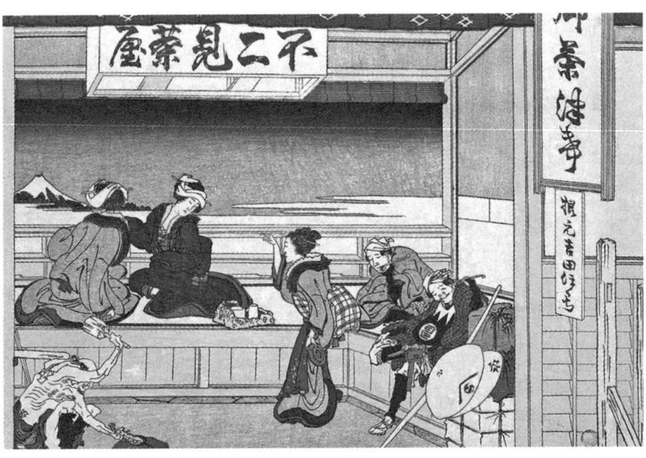

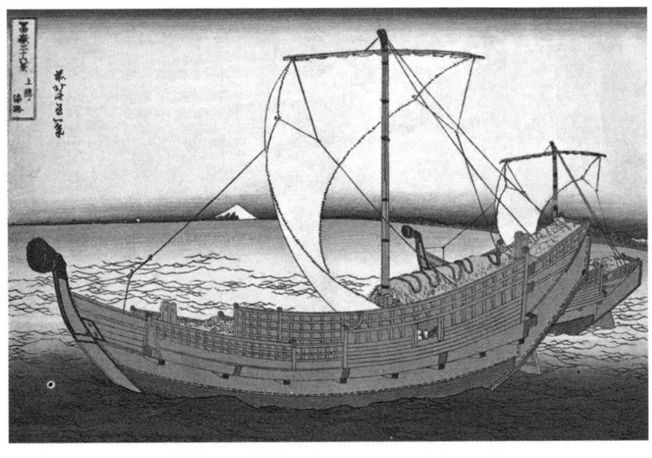

View 31
Nihonbashi Bridge in Edo

Hokusai applies Western principles of perspective, with a single vanishing point, to this view from the *Nihonbashi* (« Bridge of Japan »), the starting point of the *Gokaido⁻* (« Five Highways of Edo »): Tōkaidō, Nakasendō (or Kisō Kaidō), Koshū Kaidō, Ōshūkaidō and Nikkō Kaidō. In the distance, above the vanishing point of the buildings, Nijō Castle stands out against a layer of mist; behind it, Mount Fuji.

View 32
The Village of Sekiya on the Sumida River

Hunched over their horses, their clothes flying in the wind, messengers gallop along a winding dyke through the marshes outside the village of Sekiya. A tall, twisted pine marks the way, and on the noticeboard to the right are official proclamations and edicts.

View 33
Noboto Bay

On a beach in what is now Tokyo Bay, fishermen and women from the village of Noboto eagerly fill their baskets with clams beneath the *torii* of a Shinto shrine dedicated to a god of the sea. From the distance, Mount Fuji discreetly observes this cheerful scene in which human beings seem to be in perfect harmony with nature.

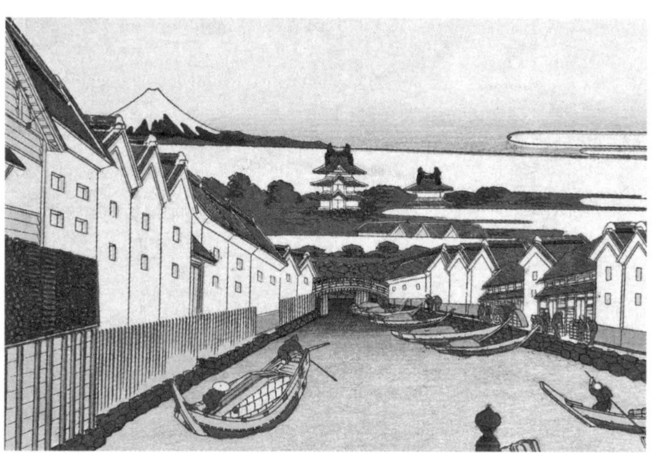

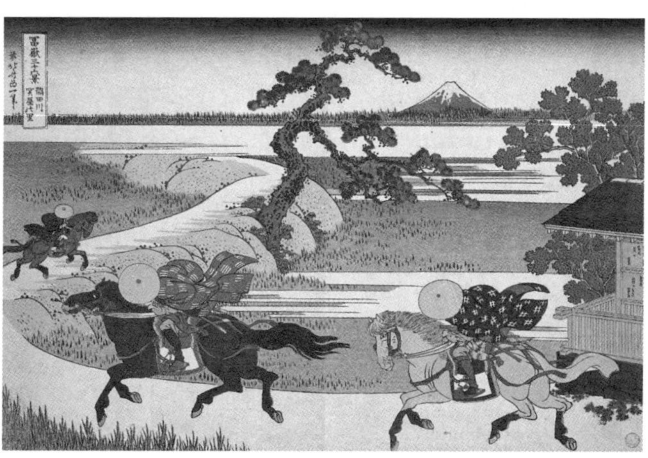

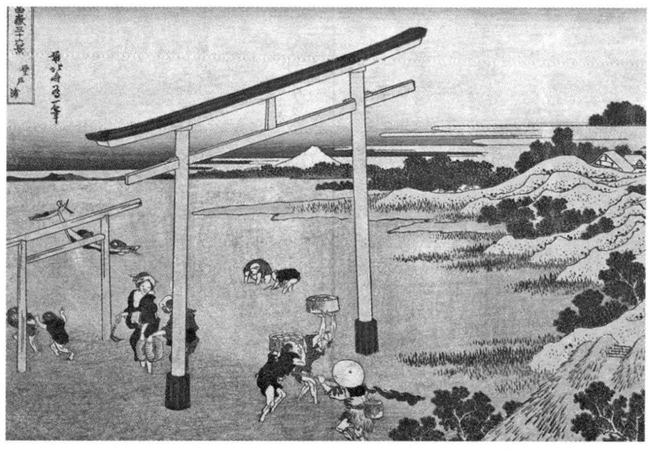

View 34
Hakone Lake in Sagami Province

The mountainous Hakone region, east of Mount Fuji, is a treacherous
part of the Tōkaidō, but here Hokusai presents a peaceful scene, with
Hakone (or Ashinoko) Lake surrounded by gentle hills and shrouded
in pink mist. The Prussian blue roofs by the lake represent the Hakone
Shrine.

View 35
*Reflection in Lake Kawaguchi, seen from the Misaka Pass
in Kai Province*

In this view of the Misaka Pass and Lake Kawaguchi, fringed by the
thatched houses of a mountain village, Hokusai takes up the theme of
the seasons as a symbol of the eternal renewal of life. The reflection of
a snow-capped Mount Fuji contrasts with the bare rocky summit above.

View 36
Hodogaya on the Tōkaidō

Near Hodogaya, the 18th Station of the Tōkaidō, the path is lined with
pines. Two porters cool off in the shade, while a traveller on horseback
has just passed a monk – with his straw hat, bamboo flute and begging
bowl – walking the other way.

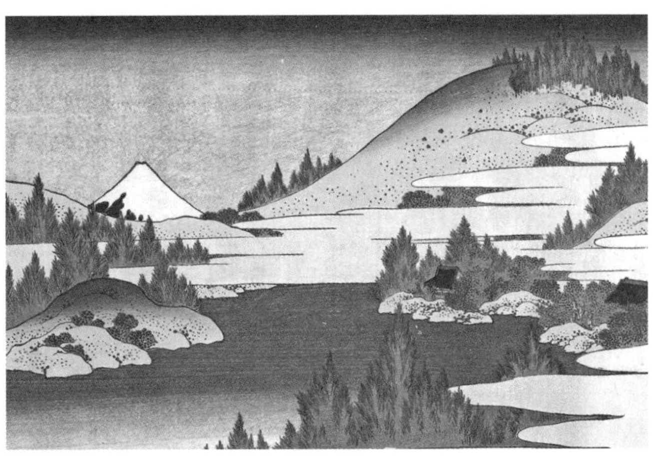

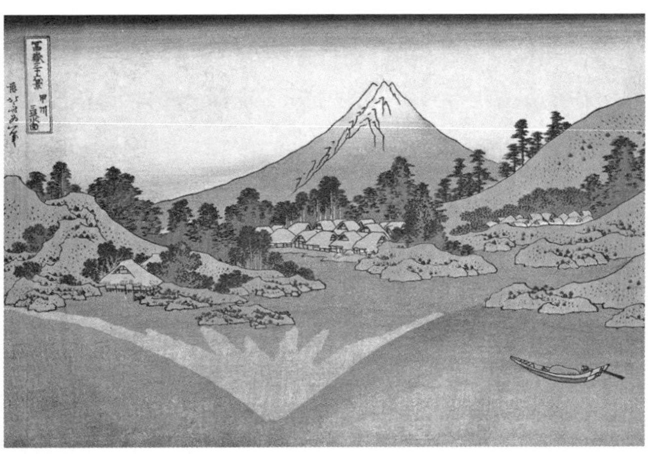

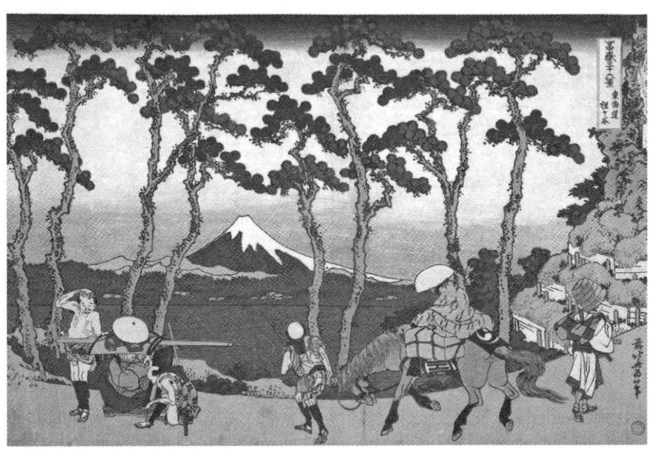

View 37
Honjo on the Tatekawa

Three carpenters are at work on a construction site in Honjo, on the banks of the Tatekawa, a canal linking northern Edo with the Sumida estuary. The writing on the planks in the foreground – the name of the publisher (Nishimura) and « New Edition of Thirty-Six Views of Mount Fuji », as well as the name and address of the sawmill – indicate that this is the first of the 10 supplementary views that Nishimura Yohachi commissioned from Hokusai after the initial publication of the series.

View 38
Mount Fuji Seen from the « Pleasure District » of Senju

Near the so-called Pleasure District of Senju (in the background), a group of daimyo (feudal lords) enters the village – the first Station of the Nikkō Kaidō, north-east of Edo – carrying guns wrapped in red cloth. Two women sit watching with interest in a field that has just been harvested, indicating that this is an autumnal scene. At the head of the long procession of samurai, the most senior daimyo, in a palanquin, pauses in front of a tea house.

View 39
Goten Hill at Shinagawa on the Tōkaidō

Local *chōnin* and passers-by celebrate the arrival of spring with the traditional *hanami* (« cherry blossom viewing ») on Goten Hill near Shinagawa. The pale pink blossom contrasts with the green countryside dotted with blue-roofed tea houses. On the far side of Sagami Bay, Mount Fuji is silhouetted against a clear sky, its slopes accented in Prussian blue.

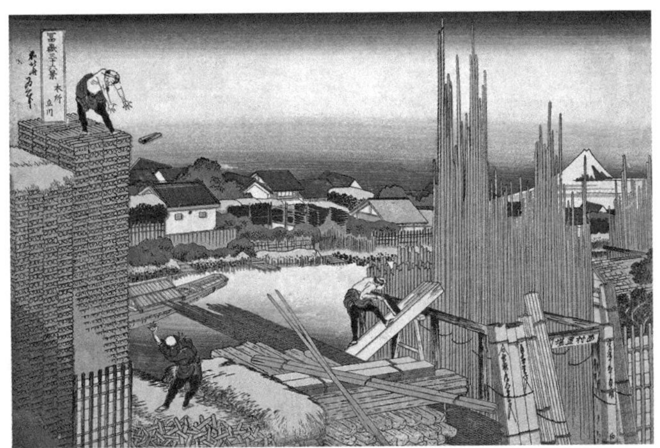

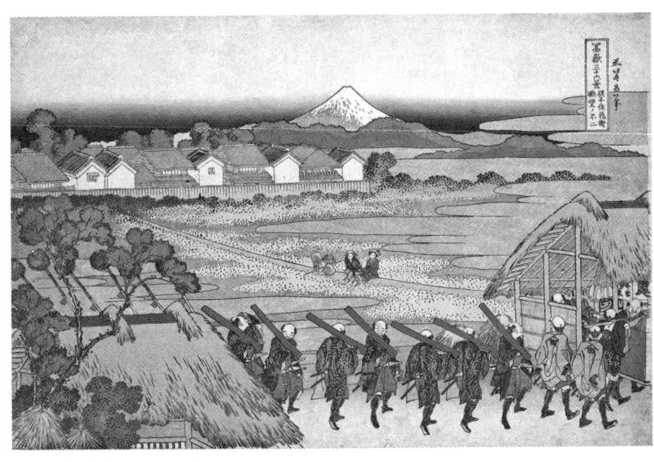

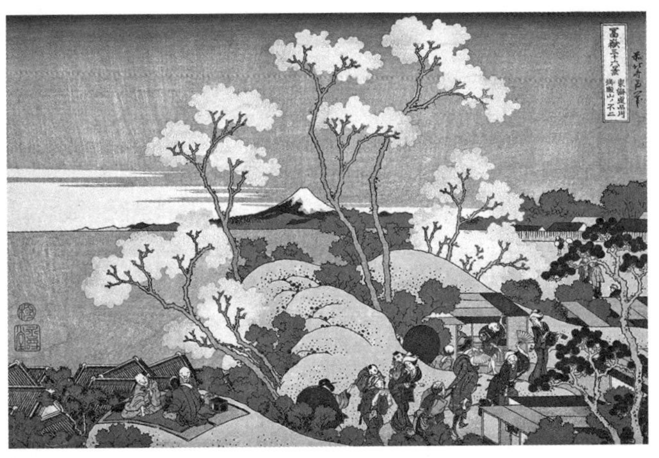

View 40
Nakahara in Sagami Province

Pilgrims, peasants, travellers and traders rub shoulders on a narrow country road in the Nakahara district. The man on the right, probably a trader, pauses to look at Mount Fuji. On his back are a rolled umbrella and a large box wrapped in a green *furoshiki* showing his company's logo. On the left, a fisherman hunches over a basket, while a woman carries a baby on her back and food on her head – possibly for her husband working in the fields.

View 41
Dawn at Isawa in Kai Province

Dominating the village of Isawa, Mount Fuji emerges from dense fog that lends the image a phantasmagorical atmosphere. The great volcano, still dark against the early morning sky, seems to float above the river, like a god looking down upon us from the clouds. In the foreground, Isawa is already alive with traders and travellers making an early start.

View 42
The Back of Fuji from the Minobu River

Traders, travellers and peasants make their way along the Minobu river. In the centre of the picture, a man leading two horses is about to pass a *kago* (a kind of rudimentary palanquin made of bamboo and slung beneath a single pole, carried by two men). In the background, the north face of Mount Fuji is framed by two impressive crags.

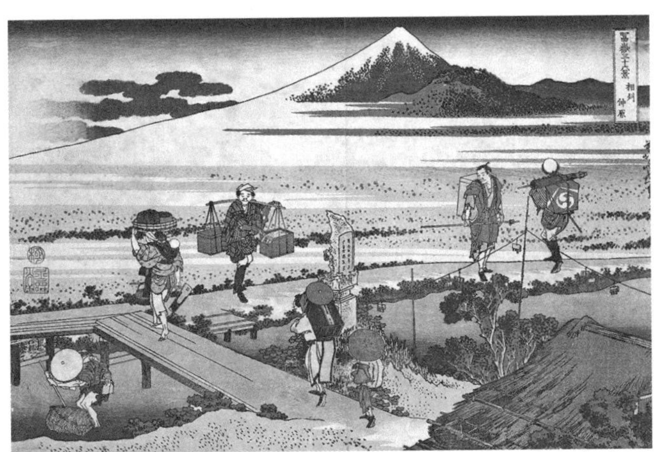

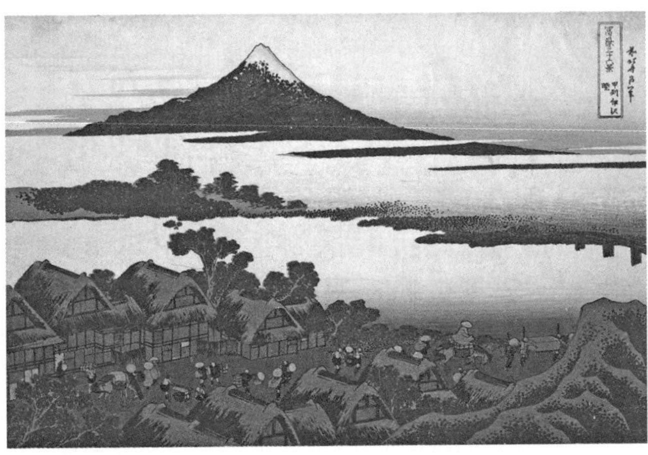

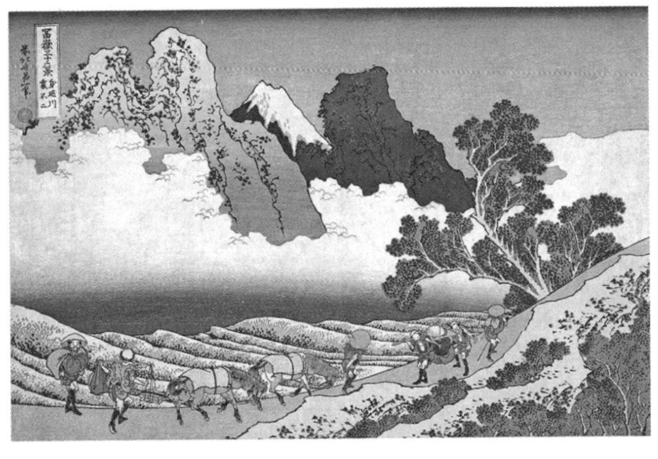

View 43
New Rice Fields at ōno in Suruga Province

Egrets fly over misty rice fields at Ōno, while five massive oxen, laden
with great sheaves of reeds, are led by peasants with their straw hats
dangling behind them. At the front of the little procession, two women
carry heavy loads – probably of fruit they have picked.

View 44
Mount Fuji from the Tea Plantation in Katakura in Suruga Province

Mount Fuji, almost completely covered in snow, is seen from a tea plantation in the district of Katakura. Women harvest the tea, while men
carry large bins full of leaves along winding paths to the store room. In
the foreground, a groom tries to lead a reluctant horse across a bridge
to unload the four bins it is carrying.

View 45
Fuji from Kanaya on the Tōkaidō

Loin-clothed porters brave the fast-flowing waters of the *Ōi river* to
transport goods, palanquins and individual travellers between Kanaya,
on the Tōkaidō, to the village of Shimada. The green cloth over the box
on the left, marked *kotobuki* («long life»), contains clothing – no doubt
belonging to the future bride of a Shimada man ...

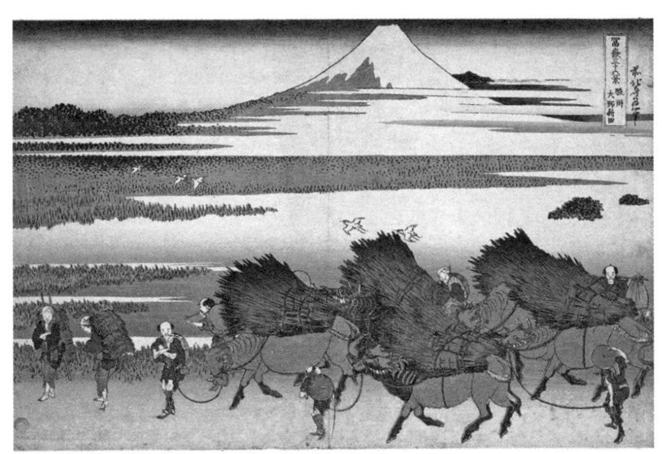

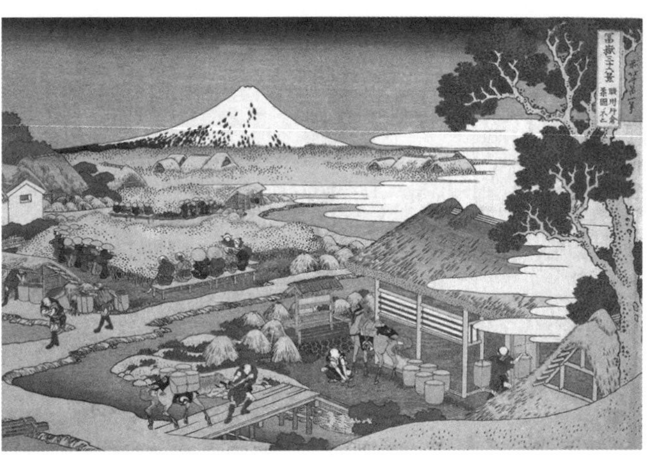

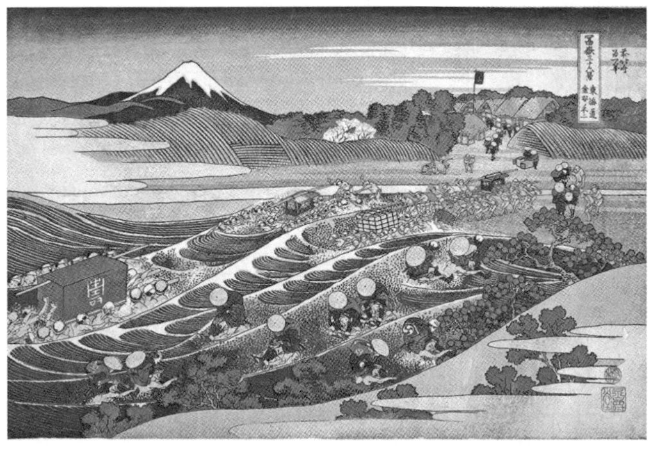

View 46
Ascending Mount Fuji

Warmed by the early morning sun – indicated by the pink streaks in the
sky – pilgrims make their way up the rocky slopes of Mount Fuji, which
are home to a number of Shinto and Buddhist shrines. One such grotto,
high on the right, is already crowded with ardent worshippers.

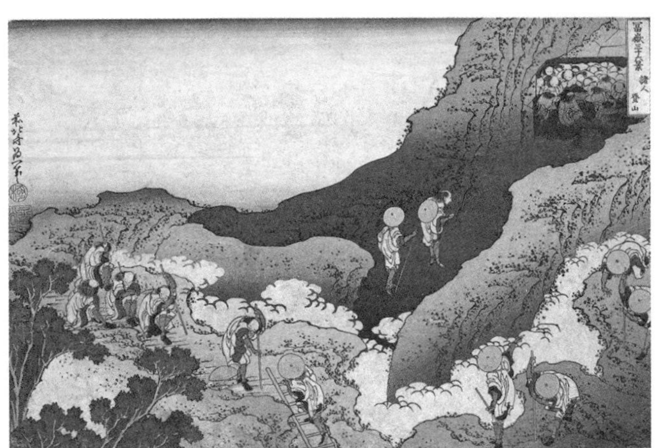

Photo credits

The Metropolitan Museum of Art, New York – all images except p. 34:
© 2018. Fine Art Images/Heritage Images/Scala, Florence

The author would like to thank everyone at Éditions Hazan, as well as Anne-Isabelle Vannier, Jérôme Gille and Marie-Hélène Durand at Corbiac, for their encouragement and support; her colleague and friend Pierre Hamard for his kindness and helpful advice; Julie Richaud and Charlène Boulay for their love and loyalty; Renaud Bezombes for his careful editing; and Laurence Mignon, Maryse Manach and Frédéric Wronski.

© Prestel Verlag, Munich · London ·
New York, 2019. Reprinted 2024
A member of Penguin Random House
Verlagsgruppe GmbH
Neumarkter Strasse 28 · 81673 Munich

The original edition was published under
the title *Hokusai. Les Trente-Six Vues du mont Fuji* at Édition Hazan, 2018.
© Éditions Hazan, 2018

Library of Congress Control Number is
available; a CIP catalogue record for this
book is available from the British Library.

Editorial direction: Julie Kiefer
Translation from French: Joseph Laredo
Proofreading: John Stilwell
Typesetting: Weiß-Freiburg GmbH –
Graphics & Book Design
Production management:
Friederike Schirge
Printing and binding: Toppan-LeeFung,
China

Printed in China

ISBN 978-3-7913-8607-2

www.prestel.com